40 SCRIPTURE BASED
PRAYERS TO PRAY OVER YOUR HUSBAND

KAYLENE YODER

HUMBLE
WISE
PRESS

ISBN: 978-0-9996380-0-2 (print), 978-0-9996380-1-9 (epub)

This book is the "just prayers" edition of
A Wife's 40-Day Fasting and Prayer Journal,

which provides a additional coaching through daily devotions,
Scripture writing assignments, and fasting techniques.

Publishing and Design Services | MartinPublishingServices.com

Stock Photography: 123rf.com
Contributors: alga38, anamomarques, anskuw, azalia, belchonock, chris_elwell, egal, erostunova, karandaev, kellyplz, kuzmichstudio, loonara, lyulka12, mashe, neirfy, pat138241, photoauris, photoncatcher, prakobkit, saddako, serazetdinov, sinseeho, stephaniefrey, steve_byland, szefei, Taiga, teerawit, tepikina, tomnamon, tuvi, valery_potapova, varts, vladir09, wollertz, yasonya,

CONTENTS

DEDICATION

For my Sam

Through it all,
you're still the one
I choose to
laugh with,
pray for,
love.

INTRODUCTION

Do you know you hold a powerful position as a wife? I didn't, until I had nowhere to turn except to the Lord. As I cried out to Him from my pit of frustrations and brokenness, He wrapped me in His love and gave me strength to take just one more step. He taught me how to live dependent upon Him by displaying His faithfulness to me. He re-centered my hope solidly in Himself, then enabled me to live through His empowering love and grace.

My first cries for help were mostly incomprehensible between the tears, sniffles, and sobs. But the One who knows me inside and out proved that He is not so far that He cannot hear, nor is He so lofty that He will not hold His broken daughter. I needed help. I needed healing. My soul reached for its Maker and he answered.

Over the years, I have had many messy conversations with our Heavenly Father. At times I have cried, "Where are You?" or, "What do You think You're doing? Why don't You show up?" To which He has answered, "Wait, My child. It's not time yet. Beautiful things will come of this; even greater than you can imagine."

Other times I have run to Him with so much praise and thanksgiving that I thought my poor human heart might burst. And I could feel Him smiling over me and whispering, "I love you, too, sweet one."

In His personal, Fatherly way the Lord encourages each of us to engage in relationship with Him through Christ. No matter where we are, how far we've fallen, or how desperate our situation, He invites us to come boldly before the throne of grace and present our needs to Him. Large or small, prayer after prayer, keep bringing your requests before Him. He has His eye on His faithful ones, never tiring of their appearances before Him.

Sweet friend, I don't know what your marriage holds right now. Maybe you are distraught and overwhelmed; your heart in shambles. Possibly you are engaged or newly married and you desire to place your husband and marriage in the Father's hands from the very beginning. Or maybe this praying idea is your last resort – it was mine at one time, too. Whatever your story, my guess is you have a mustard seed of faith somewhere that is ready to move the mountains, whether seen or unseen, in Jesus' name.

As you pray through this book, I trust you will see God working mightily in your marriage. I pray He would pour out His love and grace over you, restoring the broken pieces of your life and making you like a well-watered garden, vibrant, complete, and nourished in Him. I pray you will never grow weary of hearing your knees hit the floorboards before the Lord and that you would "always pray and never give up" (Luke 18:1). Because when you turn to the Father with your open, humble heart He will raise you up stronger, wiser, and more confident in Him.

Take this book of prayers with you wherever you go. Use it to help you pray in any spare moment of your day – in traffic jams, the waiting room, your children's sporting events, on your knees beside your bed – wherever you are, be looking for a moment to connect with Your Comforter and Guide. Then watch Him work great things in your heart and your marriage.

May our Father, who art in Heaven, supply your every need, anointing you with His peace and His joy as you walk in all power and authority in Jesus' name, Amen.

Proverbs 31:29-30

"Many women
do noble things,
but you surpass them all.
Charm is deceptive,
and beauty is fleeting;
but a woman who
fears the Lord
is to be praised."

PRAYING FOR YOU, HIS WIFE

The heart of her husband
doth safely trust in her,
so that he shall have
no need of spoil.
She will do him
good and not evil
all the days of her life.

Proverbs 31:11-12 KJV

Proverbs 12:4
1 Peter 3:1-2
Philippians 4:5-7

Father God, thank You for this man you have given me. Thank you for how far You have brought us. You have proven to be faithful, ever present, and good. Oh, so good. My heart overflows with praise and thanksgiving to You.

Reflecting on our marriage, I am convicted that I haven't always been the wife You designed me to be, nor the wife my husband needs. I confess the times I have been disrespectful in words, attitudes, and deeds. I see them as You do: sin. Remove any bitterness, selfishness, and impatience from my heart. In those places plant ready forgiveness, patience, and the willingness to bear all things.

Make me kind, Lord. Make me gentle and good. Teach me Your ways. Transform my heart into a sensitive, grace-extending one. Make me faithful, not only in body, but also in the way I speak and behave toward my husband. Make me the kind of wife who will not do or say anything to degrade or devalue my husband, but one who is trustworthy. Renew my mind so I can judge my words and actions based on Your truth and not just by how I feel. Let my husband know that I will bring him good and not evil all the days of my life (Proverbs 31:11).

Father, I know my first and foremost ministry is to my husband. Remind me of this often throughout the day. Help me seek ways to bless my husband with my body, words, and actions. When words are inappropriate, guard my tongue. Help me discern and choose when to speak and when to remain quiet, pointing him to You through the purity and reverence of my life (1 Peter 3:1-2). Help me understand that sometimes my words are wrong, no matter how right I am.

Transform me, Lord. Remind me not to expect my husband to fulfill me in ways only You can. Help me lay all my expectations at Your feet instead of his. Help me accept him the way he is and not try to change him into what I want him to be. At the same time, I release him to You to be molded, shaped, and grown into the man You created him to be: a man so much greater than I could ever hope to make him.

Father, work in me daily, that I might become the wife of my husband's dreams, one he can love easily, trust fully, laugh with, cry with, and grow old with. Give him a new wife, and let it be me. Oh, Lord, let it be me - completely transformed, fitting perfectly into the plan You have for his life and our marriage. Amen.

Trust
Scripture Readings

Psalm 143:6-12

Psalm 56:3-13

Psalm 91:1-8

Psalm 91:9-16

Psalm 121:1-8

Psalm 73:21-28

Psalm 145:13-21

Hebrews 13:5-8

Isaiah 8:11-17

Psalm 25:1-5

PROTECTING
YOUR MARRIAGE

Unite us, Father.
Give us one mind
and one spirit.
Make our marriage
a blessing to us.

Amen.

Romans 12:3
Romans 15:5
Ephesians 4:2-3
1 Corinthians 1:10

Jesus, thank You for the perfect picture of marriage through Your relationship with the church. Help us replicate that model in ways glorifying to You. Teach us to love one another and "make every effort to do what leads to peace and to mutual edification" (Romans 14:19).

Father, don't let us grow apart or become comfortable in going our own ways, but bring unity between us so that we may be like-minded toward one another (Romans 15:5). I lift our marriage to You, asking that You refine us to be "perfectly united in mind and thought" (1 Corinthians 1:10).

Lord, I pray our commitment to You and to each other will grow stronger every day, binding together a tie that is not easily broken. Infuse us with the power of love in its purest form. Teach us to be kind to one another, tenderhearted, forgiving one another, just as we are forgiven in Christ (Ephesians 4:32). Let us not grow weary of doing good to each other, so that at just the right time we may reap an abundant harvest (Galatians 6:9).

Lord, I pray You will protect us from anything that could harm or destroy our marriage. When trials persist, bring out of them a stronger marriage and faith. Let nothing come into our hearts, minds, and actions that could threaten our marriage. I take a stand against the enemy's schemes to divide us through the lusts of the eyes and flesh. Open our discernment to recognize bitterness, jealousy, irritation, doubt, distrust or the like, and not let them grow into full blown division of our marriage.

Unite us, Father. Give us one mind and one spirit. Make our marriage a blessing to us. Help us find fulfillment, meaning, purpose, and growth in our commitment to each other. Protect us, Father. Preserve and strengthen our commitment to each other and You. In Jesus' name, Amen.

PREPARING FOR YOUR MARRIAGE BED

I belong to my lover,
and his desire is for me.

Song of Solomon 7:10

Genesis 2:25
Song of Solomon 2:16
1 Corinthians 7:2-5

Father God, thank you for this man You have blessed me with. I pray You would give him an increased sense of fulfillment in our physical time together, so that he might be encouraged to flourish in all areas of his life.

Father, You have designed my husband with a need for my body. Teach me how to give myself willingly and wholeheartedly. Remind me to plan and prepare for my husband so that I might not see his needs as obligations but rather as opportunities to love deeply. Let me find sex enjoyable and fulfilling.

I pray my husband will see my physical being as a gift and that he may be satisfied and captivated by my love (Proverbs 5:19). May our marriage bed be kept pure and honorable before You. May we not defile each others' bodies. Father, I stand against any temptations to partake in extra-marital affairs or adulterous thoughts. May our trust in each other never be broken or endangered by the schemes of the enemy or evil plans of others.

I pray, Father, that You will remove any remembrances or enticements of other intimate relationships we may have had prior to our commitments to one another. Purify our minds from any wanderings or longings of past relationships. Replace them with renewed rapture and devotion to each other. As we become one in the flesh, may we bring glory to You, the Author and Creator of intimacy. In Jesus name, Amen.

GUARDING
HIS EYES

Lord,
help me be the wife
who delights her
husband's soul.

Amen.

Song of Solomon 8:10
Matthew 6:22-23
Ephesians 1:18-19

ather, we know our eyes are the lamps of our bodies. With them, we introduce either light or darkness into our hearts (Matthew 6:22-23). Give my husband the courage to guard his eyes from evil. Remove from him any desire to indulge his flesh in pornography, sexually explicit images, and crude humor. Convict him and move him to get rid of any evil-promoting practices so he will not defile himself.

Lord, I know You cannot tolerate wrong (Habakkuk 1:13). I believe that You will pour out Your wrath and spend Your anger on those who do not obey Your command to remove defiling images and idols (Ezekiel 20:7-8). Spare my husband from Your anger, and strengthen him to do as You bid in keeping his body, the temple of the Holy Spirit, pure. I pray You will be patient yet firm with my husband as You continue refining him in the area of guarding his eyes.

Jesus, I pray also that the eyes of my husband's heart will be enlightened, so that he may know the hope to which You have called him. May he see the riches of Your inheritance and Your incomparably great power, and may this knowledge move him to further seek to guard and purify his eyes, the lamp of his body (Ephesians 1:18-19).

Father, I pray now that my lover, my husband, would find fulfillment by seeing and experiencing my physical body. I pray he would be enthralled by my form, seeing only beauty and flawlessness (Song of Solomon 4:7). May I "become in his eyes like one bringing contentment" (Song of Solomon 8:10), the one who delights his soul. In Jesus' mighty name, Amen.

GUARDING HIS MIND

Do not conform any longer
to the pattern of this world,
but be transformed by the
renewing of your mind.

Romans 12:2

Romans 8:5-8
Ephesians 4:22-24
2 Corinthians 10:5
Colossians 3:1-2

Father God, You know and discern our thoughts and the intents of our hearts (Hebrews 4:12). Do not let my husband walk in ways that are not good, pursuing his own desires and imaginations. Instead, make him wise and discerning with a mind like Christ's (1 Corinthians 2:16), weighing his thoughts with the truth of Your Word.

Father, we know those who live according to the sinful nature have their minds set on what that nature desires (Romans 8:5). We also know that because evil-minded people don't think it worthwhile to retain knowledge of You, You give them over to depraved minds. They become filled with all the wicked, senseless, faithless, heartless, ruthless things they desire (Romans 1:28-31).

Father, I stand in faith, praying You will not give my husband over to depraved thoughts which can result in all kinds of diseases of the mind. I pray You remove any spirits of fear, negativity, impurity, selfishness, anger, and the like from my husband's mind. Replace such things with a sound mind, one that has the power to think rightly and justly, one that dwells on Your truth.

I pray that my husband will not be conformed to any pattern of this world, but be transformed by the renewing of his mind (Romans 12:2), taking captive every thought and making it obedient to You (2 Corinthians 10:5) so that he will be able to test and approve what is your good and perfect will in all circumstances (Romans 12:2).

Lord, I lift my husband to You to be made new in his thoughts. Convict him and enable him to stand against the enemy when an attack is made on his mind. Help him stand strong, clear-minded and self-controlled, so he can hear You when he prays (1 Peter 4:7). May he think only on things that are true, noble, right, pure, and lovely - whatever is admirable or praiseworthy - so that the peace of God, which surpasses all understanding, will be able to guard his heart and mind in Christ Jesus (Philippians 4:7-8). In Jesus' name, Amen.

A RIGHT HEART

Search me, O God,
and know my heart;
test me and know
my anxious thoughts.
See if there is any
offensive way in me,
and lead me in
the way everlasting.

Psalm 139:23-24

Psalm 86:11-12
Psalm 90:12
Psalm 119:111-112
Hebrews 4:12

Father, thank You for giving my husband a heart that is teachable. Even when he is unwilling to change his views or ways You, oh Lord, have the power to work in his heart making it pliable to Your will and Your ways. Create in my husband a new and a steadfast spirit (Psalm 51:10) for You have not given him a heart of stone but of flesh.

Your Word teaches us a good man brings good things out of the goodness of his heart, and the evil man evil things out of his heart (Luke 6:45). Let my husband stand firmly in righteousness that overflows from a heart ablaze for You. Teach him to walk in Your truth. Give him an undivided heart (Psalm 86:11), not one that entertains both good and evil.

Father, You have said, "I, the Lord, search the heart and examine the mind, to reward a man according to his conduct, according to what his deeds deserve" (Jeremiah 17:9-10). Search his heart, Jesus. Ever so gently, search his heart. Test him and know his thoughts. See if there is any offensive way in him. Convict him in any areas where he needs to grow more gentle, humble, kind, loving or repentant, then guide him into Your everlasting way (Psalm 139:23-24).

When the road gets hard, do not let his heart be troubled. Prove Yourself to my husband so his trust in You may be established, further purifying his heart by faith. May he praise You with all his heart, soul, and mind, glorifying Your name forever. In Jesus' name, Amen.

7

A GREATER FAITH

Then Jesus said to her,
"Woman, you have great faith!
Your request is granted."

Matthew 15:28

Romans 4:20-21
Hebrews 11:6
James 1:6-8
2 Timothy 1:6-7

Father, bless my husband with an extra dose of faith today. Reveal Yourself to him in mighty and undeniable ways. I pray You will be so apparent to him that his faith cannot rest on man's wisdom, but only in Your great power (1 Corinthians 2:5). May He turn to You in all he does, knowing You reward those who earnestly seek You.

Father, remind him often what You have already done for him so he doesn't forget Your faithfulness. May his faith grow to new heights as he becomes fully persuaded that You have the power to do exactly what You have said You will (Romans 4:21).

When he asks anything in Your name, help him not doubt You (James1:6-7). Where there may be a tinge of doubt, help his unbelief. Strengthen His trust in Your power, Your ways, Your ability, and Your promises. Where he is weak, display Your strength. When his faith is timid, feed him courage and boldness. Where his faith has grown complacent, renew it like a wildfire, burning and blazing - yearning for more of You. Do not let any unbelief or doubt outweigh his hope and trust in You so that at the end of his long faith-filled life, he may stand before You and confidently say, "I have fought the good fight, I have finished the race, I have kept the faith" (2 Timothy 4:7). In Jesus' Name, Amen.

8

A BETTER ATTITUDE

Father,
put a right spirit in me,
one that is ready
to do Your will
and follow Your ways.

Amen.

Ezekiel 18:31
Ezekiel 36:26-27
Philippians 2:3-8

Dear heavenly Father, thank You for giving my husband a sound mind (2 Timothy 1:7). I pray You would guard his heart and mind so his thoughts may be found pleasing in Your sight.

Father, enable my husband to steer his attitude correctly. Remind him often to humble himself before You as Jesus did, taking on the nature of a servant, willing to serve those around him in love (Philippians 2:5-8). Give him a desire to obey Your Word. Help him to be ready to do whatever is good, to avoid slander, to be peaceable and considerate in all that he does, showing true humility toward all people (Titus 3:1-2).

Jesus, it is in Your name that I take a stand against any attitudes of pride or self-righteousness that might be taking root in my husband even now. Pluck out the old mindsets and in their stead, plant new and holy ones, Father. Give him wisdom and grace to honor others before himself, always devoted to those around him in brotherly love (Romans 12:10).

Father, put a right spirit in my husband, one that is ready to follow Your will and Your ways all the days of his life. In Jesus' name, Amen.

HIS LOVE
FOR OTHERS

Father,
help me love You
more and more.
Set my heart upon You
so that I may live a life
of power and purpose.

Amen.

Romans 12:9-10
Ephesians 5:1-2
1 Corinthians 13:1-8

Father, I praise You for sending Your Son and giving us the perfect example of love: to love others the way they *need* to be loved and not how they deserve to be loved. I pray You will put such a love in my husband's heart, a love that's unselfish and doesn't expect compensation.

Father, I pray my husband will do nothing out of selfish ambition or vain conceit. but will, in humility, consider others better than himself. Teach him not to seek his own ways, or have ulterior motives when he serves others, but to be genuinely concerned about their well-being. Teach him that love is patient and kind, not envious, boastful, proud, rude or easily angered (1 Corinthians 13:4-8). Help him lay down his will and plans when it is edifying to others to do so. May he see that in humbling himself, he is not giving up or being shamed, but rather through his deference to other people, he will receive a more lasting reward in the future.

Father, soften my husband's heart toward me and our children. Teach him to give himself up for us. Give him wisdom and understanding when dealing with his children. Help him persevere in living out a patient, forgiving love. May his kindness be a beautiful model of the way You love us, making You appealing and approachable to our children. Father, also help my husband display a pure love toward me. As leader of our marriage, help him be selfless and give more than he takes. Enable him to live out of the powerful love that always trusts and always protects.

Father, I pray my husband will learn to love You more and more each day. Remind him often that neither life nor death, neither angels nor demons, neither the present nor the future, neither height nor depth, nor anything else in all creation, will be able to separate him from Your great love (Romans 8:38-39). May knowing this give him an ever increasing desire to walk in obedience to Your command to love. In Jesus' precious name, Amen.

10

FINDING JOY IN TRIALS

But I trust in
Your unfailing love;
my heart rejoices
in Your salvation.
I will sing to the Lord,
for He has been
good to me.

Psalm 13:5-6

Psalm 16:11
Psalm 30:11-12
Psalm 94:19
Habakkuk 3:18-19

Dear Heavenly Father, thank You for promising Your strength to us. We find joy in being able to rely on You when trials blaze. I pray that Your consolation during the harder times of life will be a source of joy for me and my husband. Do not let us be distraught and burdened beyond what we can bear. Let us rest in knowing You bring nothing that will harm or destroy Your faithful ones.

Father, I pray specifically for my husband, that You would teach him to see trials for what they are: the testing of his faith. Help him endure Your refining work as an examination of his belief in You. Through the trials prove to my husband that You are his strength, his source of joy, and that You enable him to go the heights (Habakkuk 3:18-19) Father, when he has remained steadfast in You, complete his joy as he looks back and sees growth and maturity in himself (James1:2-4).

Help my husband ever trust in You, Father, no matter what storm or season he faces. When life is easy for a time, help my husband see it as a gift from You. Help him not take it for granted, but continue to prepare his heart and mind with Your Word. When he is crossing turbulent waters, teach him Your unfailing love so he will not be shaken. Grant him eternal blessings and make him glad with the joy Your presence (Psalm 21:6-7). In Jesus' name, Amen.

CLAIMING PEACE

Great peace
have they who
love Your law,
and nothing can
make them stumble.

Psalm 119:165

Numbers 6:24-26
Isaiah 26:3
Philippians 4:6-7

Dear Heavenly Father, in this world we are promised trouble, yet in You, we are promised peace. We take heart in the knowledge that You have overcome the world (John 16:33), and that in You we may have peace at all times and in every way (2 Thessalonians 3:16).

Father, when darts of the evil one are being fired from all directions, keep my husband's mind steadfast on You desiring Your peace and Your presence. Help him to not be anxious about anything, but in everything, make his requests known to You by prayer and petition (Philippians 4:6-7). Impart peace beyond measure upon him, reassuring him that You are not slack in Your promises. May Your blessed assurance keep him from succumbing to the temptations of despair, hopelessness, depression, or distrust in You.

Father, move my husband's heart to also promote peace in all he does by not being quick to argue or seek revenge. It is to a man's honor to avoid strife, but every fool is quick to quarrel (Proverbs 20:3). Lord, You have not made my husband to be a fool, but a man of courageous faith. Help him be kind, patient, and loving, making every effort to do what leads to peace and mutual edification of those around him (Romans 14:19).

May my husband's heart overflow with Your peace, Father, and spill out of his life for all to see. I ask that You now give him a desire to love You and want to serve You more and more each day. In Jesus' name, Amen.

12

GROWING
IN PATIENCE

Be completely
humble and gentle;
be patient, bearing with
one another in love.

Ephesians 4:2

James 1:2-4
Colossians 1:9-12
Proverbs 15:18
1 Thessalonians 5:14

Father, thank You for being a patient God. Thank You that Your mercies are never ending. I pray You will give my husband a heart that is patient and understanding, one that will go the distance of bearing with others.

Your Word tells us a man's wisdom gives him great patience and that it is to his glory to overlook an offense (Proverbs 19:11). Anoint him with wisdom and help him choose patience in all circumstances.

Father, convict my husband to let go of any impatience, grudges, anger, jealous tendencies or harsh words. In their place, teach him to be completely humble and gentle, bearing with others in love (Ephesians 4:2). When people are difficult or plans don't turn out as expected, give him an accepting attitude. Help him see that Your way is never wrong and that the testing of his faith will invariably include the testing of his patience. Help him clothe himself with kindness and compassion (Colossians 3:12-13),and persevere in doing what is good.

Fill my husband with the knowledge of Your will through all spiritual wisdom and understanding. I stand praying that by Your power he will live a life worthy of You. May he please You in every way: bearing fruit in every good work, growing in the knowledge of God, and being strengthened according to Your glorious might so that he may have great endurance to run the race marked out before him (Colossians 1:9-11). In Jesus' precious name, Amen.

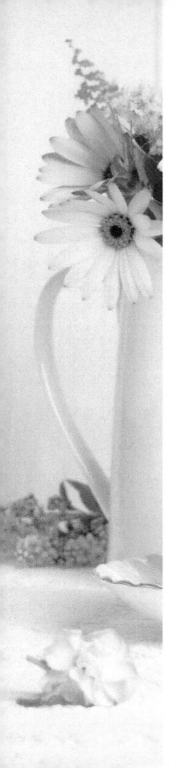

PRACTICING KINDNESS

Lord,
place Your kindness
in me today.
Help me speak gently
and love abundantly.

Amen.

Proverbs 14:31
Proverbs 31:26
1 Thessalonians 5:15
2 Peter 1:5-8

Father, thank You for Your kindness. Your mercies are never ending, reaching even to the ungrateful and wicked. Teach my husband to be kind to others, to love his enemies and do good to them (Luke 6:35). May he never pay back wrong for wrong, but always be kind to all people (1 Thessalonians 5:15).

Father, I pray You would move my husband's heart to rid himself of any bitterness, rage, anger, brawling, slander or any other form of malice. In their stead grow him to be kind and compassionate toward others, forgiving others as You have forgiven him (Ephesians 4:31-32). May he not have ulterior motives for being kind, but may true compassion permeate his words and actions.

I pray that You would prosper my husband and greatly reward his upright and pure life, Father. Your Word says a kind man benefits himself (Proverbs 11:17). May my husband benefit long term peace of mind and good reputation. May he be a workman approved by God, not being made ashamed of the ways he deals with others. In Jesus' name, Amen.

BECOMING GOOD

This is what the Lord says:
"Stand at the crossroads
and look; ask for the
ancient paths, and ask
where the good way is,
and walk in it, and you will
find rest for your souls."

Jeremiah 6:16

1 Peter 2:12
Proverbs 22:1
1 Thessalonians 5:21-22

Dear Jesus, thank You for the good You have shown my husband throughout his life. Thank you for the times You kept him from making bad choices; the times You intervened to save His life, soul, and reputation. Let him see that the favor that has come to him is not of his own doing, but from You.

Father, I pray my husband will not seek his own good or be selfish in his motives, but that he would seek the greater good of those around him (1 Corinthians 10:24). May he work toward mutual edification in all situations, so that even pagans can see Your work of goodness through him (1 Peter 2:12). Father, I pray You would impress upon him to lead a disciplined life and be clear minded and self-controlled. May he not grow weary in doing what is right, for at the proper time You promise a harvest if he doesn't give up (Galatians 6:9-10).

Father, teach my husband to seek You first and by the constant use of your Word, train himself in godliness. When he is at the crossroads of good and evil, pour out Your wisdom and discernment upon him so he may know the way that is good. Then, may Your peace surround him encouraging him as he goes the way of uprightness. In Jesus' name, Amen.

1

HIS FAITHFULNESS

Father,
grow our love for You
to be greater than our
love for each other,
so that we may be
strengthened and
equipped to remain
faithful to each other.

Amen

Psalm 18:25-36
Psalm 31:23
Ephesians 6:10-18
1 Corinthians 4:2

Jesus, thank You for Your faithfulness, even to the cross. You have proven to be our Rock. All Your ways are perfect and just. You, O Lord, are a compassionate and gracious God, slow to anger, abounding in love and faithfulness (Psalm 86:15).

I pray You would give my husband an abundant desire to grow in Your likeness. Teach him to be a man of courageous faith, standing for what is good and right in Your eyes. I pray he will be on his guard against anything that does not bring life and godliness. Make righteousness to be his belt and faithfulness the sash around his waist (Isaiah 11:5). Help him bear up under the armor You provide by girding himself in truth, so he may be able to discern good from evil. Help him be wise to the ways of the world and the lord of it, the enemy.

Father, give my husband the courage to apply Your standard to his life so that he may be known as a righteous man. When the road is dark before him, help him put on the shoes of peace so that he may not be frightened. May he stand strong in his faith, claiming his status in You.

Father, now I lay open our marriage before You. Help us stand strong using the Sword of the Spirit, Your Word, as our guide and protection against temptation. May we not yield to anything that could blemish our lives or compromise our marriage covenant. Help us renounce anything that does not bring honor and glory to You. Grow our love for You to be greater than our love for each other, for in that way we may be strengthened to remain faithful to each other.

Lord, I specifically lift my husband to You now. Make him a man pure in thought and deed, always being guided by Your Word so that he may live his life holy and blameless before You. May Your Word be written on the tablet of his heart so that his faithfulness to You may become more and more evident each day. In Jesus' name, Amen.

PRACTICING SELF-CONTROL

...be hospitable,
one who loves what is good,
who is self-controlled,
upright, holy, and disciplined.

Titus 1:8

Proverbs 16:32
1 Peter 1:13
Proverbs 29:11
Titus 2:12

Father God, I come before You, thankful for this man You have put in my life, this man You have called me to love, honor and help. I thank You that You have made him a man able to discern right from wrong. You have given him the power and ability to say "No" to temptations. Help him see where practicing more self-control would benefit his life. Keep renewing his mind, enlightening him, showing him Your will and Your way.

Father, as the leader of our marriage and family, I pray my husband would be a workman worthy of what You have called him to do. Remove any traits that are overbearing or quick tempered, may he not be given to drunkenness, violence, or pursue dishonest gain. In their place, restore hospitality; make him good, self-controlled, upright, holy and disciplined. Help him hold firm to Your trustworthy way (Titus 1:7-9).

Lord, we know our enemy, the devil, prowls around like a roaring lion looking for someone to devour (1 Peter 5:8). Today, I stand against his wicked schemes to make my husband fall. I proclaim that my husband, strong and in the power of Your might, can resist the plans of the evil one.

Father, I pray my husband will not be as some who sleep, spiritually speaking, but that he may remain alert and self-controlled, putting on faith and love as a breastplate, and the hope of salvation as a helmet (1 Thessalonians 5:6-8). I pray that You would strengthen and uphold my husband making him able to resist the darts of temptation fired at him.

Jesus, You are the perfect example of a man who is clear minded and self-controlled. Teach my husband to be the same: temperate, worthy of respect, faithful, loving and patient, doing what is good, showing integrity in all he does by his seriousness and soundness of speech. May those who oppose him be ashamed because they can find nothing bad to say about him. Through Your great grace, teach him to reject ungodliness and worldly passions, and to clothe himself with self-control, living an upright and godly life. In Jesus' name, Amen.

SEEKING WISDOM

Say to wisdom,
"You are my sister,"
and call understanding
your kinsman.

Proverbs 7:4

Psalm 111:10
Daniel 12:3
1 Kings 3:9
Proverbs 8:10-11

ather, You have promised to give wisdom where it is asked (James 1:5). I ask that You would give my husband a heart that can discern. Help him understand Your Word. Give him Your precepts and impart wisdom to him so he may know what is Your good and perfect will.

Father, I pray you will teach my husband to not be wise in his own eyes, doing what he wants, when he wants, or how he wants, but to always seek You first, wanting to please You above man. Help him understand that looking to You first will bring health and nourishment to his body (Proverbs 3:7-8).

Father, we know wisdom is found in those who take advice and accept instruction (Proverbs 13:10, 19:20). Make my husband one who is capable of accepting advice from others. Do not let him be so set in his ways that he will scoff in the face of others who mean well, rather let him thoughtfully and patiently consider their words. Let him not become angry and defensive, speaking harsh words that prove his heart is set in his own ways. Anoint him with wisdom and reveal truth, even when it's not what he wants to hear.

Father, deepen my husband's desire to grow in Your Word. It has been said, the holy Scriptures are able to make you wise (2 Timothy 3:15). I ask again that You would impart great wisdom to him, so he may lay a foundation of faith for generations to come. Help him be strong, and show himself a man, observing what You require and then walking in Your ways (1 Kings 2:2-4). Help him act justly, love mercy and to walk humbly before You, our unchangeable, infallible, sovereign Lord (Micah 6:8). In Jesus' name, Amen.

18

DEVELOPING INTEGRITY

The integrity of
the upright
guides them,
but the unfaithful
are destroyed
by their duplicity.

Proverbs 11:3

Dear Jesus, thank You for the perfect example of a life of integrity. You did everything with a sincere love for mankind and humble obedience to Your Father. I pray You will reveal Your goodness to my husband and give him the desire to follow in the path You have prepared.

Father, give my husband a heart that is sincere, hating what is evil, clinging to what is good (Romans 12:9). Many are the plans of a man's heart, but I pray, Lord, that the plans of my husband's heart are only noble ones. If the plans of his heart do not fit into Your will or do not line up with Your Word, do not let them come about. Keep him from doing anything that will lead to a guilty conscience or tarnished reputation. May integrity and uprightness protect him (Psalm 25:21). May he always do what is good, be serious, and have sound speech that cannot be condemned (Titus 2:7-8).

Father, I pray you would impart wisdom and prudence upon my husband so he may know and decide what is right. Should he tempted to do something not glorifying to You, help him stand strong in his faith and walk the way of integrity. May he remember that he who has clean hands and a pure heart will one day have the reward of standing in Your presence (Psalm 24:3-4). I pray my husband will be one who says as Job did, "till I die, I will not deny my integrity" (Job 27:5). May he lead a blameless life before You. In Jesus' name, Amen.

KEEPING HONEST

No one who practices deceit
will dwell in My house;
no one who speaks falsely
will stand in My presence.

Psalm 101:7

Psalm 24:3-4
Proverbs 12:22
Proverbs 19:9
1 Peter 3:10-12

Father, we know You do not lie and that You hate all things deceitful. Anyone who practices deceit will not dwell in Your house; anyone who speaks falsely will not stand before You (Psalm 101:7). It is one of the seven abominations and will not go unpunished (Proverbs 6:16). I pray You will remove from my husband any lying or deceptive tendencies. Make him a man who hates dishonesty as much as You do.

Father, I pray You would give my husband the desire to always speak truthfully and sincerely. May he refuse to let deceit spill from his lips. May he keep his oath even when it hurts (Psalm 15:4) because such a man will gain honor and respect. Teach him to let his "Yes" be "Yes" and his "No" be "No" (Matthew 5:37).

I pray he would be a man who is honest in all his dealings. You, oh Lord, detest differing weights and dishonest scales (Proverbs 20:23). Plant my husband in uprightness, so that no one may find fault in his dealings. May the intentions of his heart not be ones of deceit or ill gain.

Father, I pray that You would keep the words of his mouth and the meditations of his heart pleasing in Your sight (Psalm 19:14). May he always keep growing in You, seeking to live a life that is transparent and pure. In Jesus' name, Amen.

HUMILITY:
A WAY OF LIFE

Do not think of yourself
more highly than you ought,
but rather think of yourself
with sober judgment.

Romans 12:3

Proverbs 15:31-33
Proverbs 16:5,
Isaiah 66:2
James 4:10

ather, we know You hate the proud and love the humble. You have instructed us to not think of ourselves more highly than we ought to, but to think of ourselves with sober judgment (Romans 12:3). Grow my husband into a man who doesn't think himself better than those around him. Give him a heart that is willing to honor others above himself. Let him serve others without ulterior motives, selfish ambitions, or vain conceit; instead let him be humbly and graciously willing to contribute to the good of others (Philippians 2:3-4).

Father, teach my husband to be careful of the words he speaks of himself. You do not find boasting good or of any worth (1 Corinthians 5:6). Your Word tells us that whoever exalts himself will be humbled, and whoever humbles himself will be exalted (Matthew 23:12). Before a man's downfall, he is proud (Proverbs 18:12). Do not let my husband be a man brought to destruction, shame, or disgrace due to boastful words, selfish actions, or a proud heart. Let other men praise him and not himself (Proverbs 27:2). Let other men honor him and not himself.

Father, You have promised to supply meek men with wealth, honor, life, and wisdom (Proverbs 22:4; 11:2). So develop in him a heart that is not proud and eyes that are not haughty (Psalm 131:1). Teach him, even as he sleeps (Psalm 16:7), to be obedient and ready to do whatever is good, to slander no one and to be peaceable and considerate, showing true humility toward all men (Titus 3:1-2). May he not concern himself with things that seem great and wonderful on this earth, but instead, quiet his soul before You and put his hope in You both now and forevermore (Psalm 131:1-3) In Jesus' name, Amen.

COURAGE
FOR THE WAY

Lord,
I ask that You would give me
audacious courage to stand
for what is pleasing to You.

Amen.

Psalm 27:14
Psalm 112:7
Deuteronomy 31:6
Isaiah 12:2

Father, thank You that You will always be with us to guide us, direct us, comfort us and strengthen us. I pray that You will give my husband an extra measure of this assurance today. Help him be on his guard, stand firm in his faith and be a man of courage (1 Corinthians 16:13). Father, You have not given him a spirit of timidity, but a spirit of power, of love, and of self-discipline. Do not let him be ashamed to testify about You by choosing to stand against evil (2 Timothy 1:7-8).

Father, when my husband deals with difficult people, help him not be intimidated by them. Instead, make him strong and courageous, not fearing or being in dread of them. Remind him often that it is You who goes with him and that You will never leave him or forsake him (Deuteronomy 31:6). May he conduct himself in a manner worthy of the gospel, knowing that You will preserve his life.

When my husband is caught in difficult situations give him courage to do what is right. Help him trust You with all his heart and not lean on his own understanding (Proverbs 3:5). Do not let him grow discouraged. Instead make him willing to walk in ways that please You even when it's hard. Remind him that You notice and that You reward Your faithful servant. Make my husband a man of courage who is willing to go the extra mile, do the extra deed, be the extra good. In Jesus' name, Amen.

22

REPENTANCE AND FORGIVING OTHERS

Lord,
give me a tender heart
that is willing to forgive
first and fast.

Amen.

Isaiah 43:25
Proverbs 19:11
Proverbs 28:13
Matthew 6:14-15

Father, thank You for Your great mercy. You have shown it to all generations. You are a forgiving God; gracious and compassionate, slow to anger, abounding in love (Nehemiah 9:17). You have promised that when Your people turn from their sins and seek Your face, You will hear them and will be faithful to forgive and heal them (1 John 1:9).

Father, I pray You will give my husband a heart that willingly turns to You. Give him the courage to admit any wrong he may have done. Cultivate in him an ongoing, ever-strengthening desire to do what is good and pleasing in Your eyes. When You convict my husband, Father, also move him to humble repentance, seeing his sin as You do and fully renouncing its hold on his life.

Father, in his repentance give him Your peace so he may know that he is fully forgiven and may walk unashamedly before You. Assure him that You have removed his sin as far as the east is from the west and that You are the one Who blots out his transgressions and will remember them no more (Isaiah 43:25).

Father, as You have forgiven my husband of any confessed sin, also give him a heart to forgive others. Teach him that he must forgive in order to be forgiven and that You forgive with the same measure he forgives (Matthew 6:14-15). Soften my husband's heart toward anyone who treats him poorly, bearing with everyone in love. Be his Rock when it's hard to see past the pain, the unfairness, or the human tendency to seek revenge.

I pray also, Father, that You would heal the land of our marriage of any bitterness, hardness of heart, grudges or contention. Renew in us a willingness to be patient and understanding toward one another. Help us forgive quickly, overlooking offenses and not using them against each other. Heal us Father, and guard us in Your love. In Jesus' name, Amen.

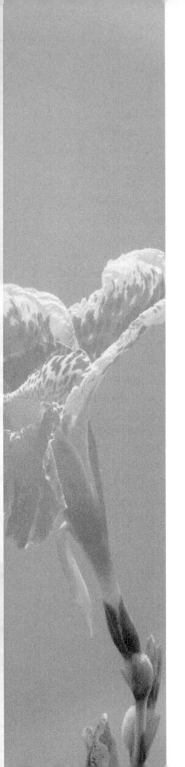

23

TRUSTING GOD
FOR HIS PROMISES

Find rest, O my soul,
in God alone,
my hope comes from Him.
He alone is my rock...

Psalm 62:5-6

Jeremiah 32:17
Hebrews 13:8
James 1:17
Psalm 56:3-4,
Psalm 119:137-138

Father, we know Your ways are good and perfect. Your Word is flawless and You promise to be a shield to those who trust in You (2 Samuel 22:31). Today I pray my husband would be dealt an extra measure of belief. Show him throughout the day that he can trust You with whatever comes. Where there is even a small measure of distrust, doubt, or trepidation, remind him that You have proven Yourself faithful since the beginning of time and You promise to remain trustworthy into all eternity.

Father, when my husband makes plans that go wrong or don't hold out, do not let him become discouraged. Remind him that this is only for a season, and that when he stands firmly on Your solid foundation and does good, You will greatly reward him. Many are the woes of the wicked, but Your unfailing love surrounds those who trust in You (Psalm 32:10). Teach my husband to know that Your thoughts and Your ways are above all others, and that You cannot allow what is not fitting to Your great plan (Isaiah 55:8-9). Let my husband rest securely in You and know that Your great and wonderful plans will prevail.

Father I pray You will also make my husband a man who can be trusted. Keep growing him in ways that are honorable, so that he may be proven by his good works as a man who is genuine and honest. I praise You, Lord, that You have given my husband a sound mind and teachable heart. Daily, speak to my husband through Your Word and Spirit. Don't let him be like fools who trust in themselves, but rather a man who walks in wisdom, his confidence secured in You (Proverbs 28:26, Jeremiah 17:7). In Jesus' name, Amen.

24

HEARING THE LORD

Lord,
incline my ear to
hear Your Word,
that I may do
as You ask.

Amen.

James 1:22
Proverbs 18:15
Matthew 7:26
Mark 4:20

Father, I praise You for the wisdom that You willingly pour out to those who ask (James 1:5). Today I pray my husband will not only ask for and seek wisdom, but that he may hear from You clearly and correctly, also. May his ears be opened, always inclined to hear Your Word; then may he do as You ask.

Jesus, You have said, "But everyone who hears these words of mine and does not put them into practice is like a foolish man who built his house on sand" (Matthew 7:26). May he never be as those who hear Your Word yet never do as it directs. You have not given my husband a heart that cannot be molded and taught, nor ears that cannot hear Your Word. Remove all foolishness and self-centered tendencies, and replace them with attitudes of love and growth.

Father, open my husband's ears to good instruction, knowledge, and sound teaching. Open his ears to words of rebuke, correction and chastisement as well. While receiving such words is never easy, it is necessary for growth. Give my husband discernment as he gives the words of correction thoughtful consideration. Make all discipline that is from You be like an ornament of fine gold to his listening ears (Proverbs 25:12). Help him recognize advice given in love and take action on anything that needs improvement.

Father, I pray all sound guidance and insight will fall on the good soil of his heart. Help him hear Your words, accept Your words, and produce an abundant harvest through his obedience to You (Mark 4:20). In Jesus' precious name, Amen.

OBEDIENCE WHEN CALLED

And this is love:
that we walk in obedience
to His commands.

2 John 6

Psalm 119:88
John 14:23
Deuteronomy 13:3-4
Deuteronomy 30:9-10

Sweet Jesus, You are a gentle presence. You are kind. You are patient. You are loving. You are also sovereign and cannot tolerate the sin of disobedience. Prove Yourself trustworthy to my husband that he may learn to love and obey Your commands without hesitation.

Lord, we know You test us to see whether we love You with all our heart and soul (Deuteronomy 13:3-4). Gently test my husband, but do not overwhelm him. When walking through times of testing grant him the peace that passes all understanding, reminding him that he is not alone in this journey.

Father, do not let my husband grow angry at You or weary of Your will. I pray he will obey the commands and decrees You have written to us and that he will turn to You with all his heart and all his soul. When doubt knocks, give him the courage to stand strong and say, "I will obey my God's teaching." Then, in due time, bless him abundantly for his devotion to You.

Father, I pray also that my husband's example of humble obedience will direct the course of his children's lives and many generations after them. Today, freshen his faith and his resolve to serve You and bring his life in compliance with Your will. In Jesus' precious name, Amen.

HIS SPIRITUAL LEADERSHIP

Lord,
help me lead my life
in ways that will
refresh and encourage
my husband.

Amen.

Deuteronomy 11:18-21
Proverbs 14:1
Mark 10:42-45
1 Timothy 5:8

Father, I praise You for the wisdom You have given my husband. Teach him to love Your Word more and more so that he will be able to lead his children in the same way.

Where spiritual leadership was not modeled for him, provide godly role models for him to fashion his life after. Teach him through Your Word that true leadership is pure and kind, not harsh or demanding. Impress upon him that a great leader will not try to "lord it over" or force his will onto those around him. Whoever wants to become great among people must be a servant or helper to all. Deepen his desire to portray Christ, who came to serve and offer up his life for others (Mark 10:42-45).

Father, strengthen my husband's faith so that he may lead diligently. Keep him rooted and built up in Christ, overflowing with thankfulness to You. Teach him to weigh all matters, and see to it that no one takes him captive through hollow or deceptive philosophy. Enlighten him so he will know what the vain, human traditions and principles of the world are rather than the teachings of Christ (Colossians 2:6-8).

Father, do not let him be intimidated by the call You have given him as spiritual leader of his home. Rather, give him the courage, ability, and ease to talk about Your words while sitting at home, walking along the road, lying down or getting up (Deuteronomy 6:6-7, 11:18-21). I pray that You would give him a renewed burden to train his children in the way they should go so that when they are old they will not depart from it (Proverbs 22:6).

Father, I pray my husband would stand strong in the power of Your might. The fear of You, oh Lord, leads to life. Do not let him stray. Should he grow slack, pursue hard after him. Do not let him wane in his faith but keep him always prepared to do what you require. May Your ways and what is edifying to growth be what comes out of his mouth first. May he lead with wisdom, integrity and servant-hood in his home, workplace, friendships, and marriage. In Jesus' precious name, Amen.

27

PURPOSEFUL FATHERHOOD

Lord,
give my husband
Your heart
toward his children.

Amen.

Ephesians 6:4
Colossians 3:21
Proverbs 22:6
Isaiah 40:11

Father in heaven, thank You for a beautiful picture of what true fatherhood looks like; not harsh yet commanding respect, not demanding yet expecting obedience, not irrational in ways that exasperate Your children but always loving, always kind, and ever gracious. Give my husband Your heart toward his children. Make him a man who communicates unconditional love to them. May they always know their father loves them and does all that he does for their good.

Help him be patient with his children, Father. Show him the grace You have covered him with so that he may, in turn, extend grace to his children. When he feels impatient, help him rise above the immediate circumstances, enabling him to speak and respond in ways he won't regret. Help him speak with calmness and authority, never letting his children doubt his love for them.

Father, show my husband where he can cultivate a deeper relationship with each child. I pray he will not be cold, harsh, uninterested, undependable, or neglectful. May he never provoke his children to wrath, but bring them up in the training and admonition of You, Lord (Ephesians 6:4). Help him be present physically and emotionally, not being ruled by what he might deem of greater importance right at that moment.

Where he feels inadequate to teach his children Your ways, give him courage and the ability to speak what they need to hear. Help him communicate Your ways to them. May the knowledge that their father loves the Almighty have a profound impact on their lives.

Father, we know You discipline those You love (Proverbs 3:12). You do it with great love, mercy, and the desire grow us up in You. When disciplining his own children, help my husband do it calmly, justly, and lovingly, never in anger, irritation or self-righteousness. Help him be a fair judge, not dealing with them in haste.

Father, I pray you will teach him, guide him, and direct his paths in this role of fatherhood. May it be one of great fulfillment to him, and when he is old and gray may he rest, knowing he obediently left a rich spiritual inheritance for his children. In Jesus' precious name, Amen.

10 Psalms for Godly Character

LOVE
Psalm 86:1-17

JOY
Psalm 16:1-11

PEACE
Psalm 23:1-6

PATIENCE
Psalm 62:1-12

KINDNESS
Psalm 116:1-19

GOODNESS
Psalm 18:1-36

FAITHFULNESS
Psalm 143:1-12

SELF-CONTROL
Psalm 37:1-11

WISDOM
Psalm 1:1-6

HUMILITY
Psalm 51:1-19

28

THE LABOR
OF HIS HANDS

Whatever you do,
work at it with all your heart,
as working for the Lord
and not for men...

Colossians 3:23

1 Chronicles 28:20
Ecclesiastes 5:18-19
1 Timothy 5:8
1 Thessalonians 4:11-12

Father, bless my husband's work. Thank you for giving him the abilities to do the work You have called him to. Help him find a proper balance between working too much and being too lazy to take on his responsibilities.

Father, I pray he may work with his own hands so that he will not grow completely dependent on anybody (1 Thessalonians 4:11-12). I pray he will make it his ambition to lead a quiet and simple life so that his daily work may win the respect of outsiders. Teach him to bring You into every aspect of his work. Where there is anything not glorifying to You, convict him, then supply him with the courage to make any necessary changes. Teach him to commit whatever he does to You, so his plans may succeed (Proverbs 16:3).

Lord, I know so much of a man is tied up in his work. Give my husband a sense of fulfillment from the labor of his life. "Nothing is better for a man than to enjoy his work, because that is his lot" (Ecclesiastes 3:22). Give him clear direction of Your plan. Help him to see past the dollar signs and rest secure knowing that Your provision will always be enough.

Father, I pray for the individuals You bring into my husband's life through his work. May they be people of integrity who encourage and strengthen his walk with You. Guide my husband away from anyone or anything that could harm his livelihood. You guide the hearts of kings like a stream (Proverbs 21:1), so I know You are capable of steering my husband away from bad business deals, jobs, or influences that could rob what he has worked for.

Father, help me to not come in the way of Your will regarding my husband's work. I confess the times I haven't been supportive or appreciative of him. Help me accept his job, knowing You are in control, guiding and prospering his efforts. You have promised hope and a future for us and our family, to prosper us and not to harm us (Jeremiah 29:11). I firmly hold on to that promise. Give me words that will encourage and affirm even when I struggle with his calling.

Father, lead him, guide him, and direct him. Then surround him, encourage him, and enable him to do his life's work humbly, willingly, and thoroughly. May he be strong and courageous, willing to do the work you call him to. In Jesus' name, Amen.

Courage
Scripture Readings

Psalm 46:1-7

Joshua 1:1-9

Matthew 10:26-31

1 Corinthians 15:56-58

2 Timothy 1:6-12

Isaiah 12:1-6

1 Kings 2:1-4

Deuteronomy 31:1-8

Psalm 27:1-6

Psalm 27: 7-14

29

HANDLING HIS FINANCES

Humility and fear
of the Lord bring
wealth and honor and life.

Proverbs 22:4

Ecclesiastes 5:10
Psalm 62:10
Proverbs 28:20
Malachi 3:10

Dear Jesus, thank You that You have provided an income for my husband. Through his work, You have always provided enough. Sometimes just enough, most times more than enough. But always, enough.

I pray now that my husband will choose wisely how to spend the money You have blessed him with. Show him where unwise spending needs to be eliminated, so finances can be freed up to pay for necessary things. May he spend his money carefully and with foresight so that he and his family will not perish (Psalm 49:20).

Father, remind him to bring the whole tithe into the storehouse before he spends Your money elsewhere. You have promised that when we are faithful in returning to You what You ask, You will throw open the floodgates and pour out so much blessing that we will not have room enough for it all (Malachi 3:10).

Father, create in my husband an honest heart when it comes to earning money. I pray You will far remove any thought or consideration that will lead to extortion, stealing, or dishonest financial gain in any way. May he never bring punishment upon his own head or his family by being eager to get rich (Proverbs 28:20). Remove from him any tendency toward greediness or selfish financial advancement, and replace it with contentment and satisfaction with what You have provided.

Father, with any extra money, give my husband a desire to bless others and give freely from the overflow. Don't let him become reckless or selfish with his money. May he always know that You are the Provider and Giver of every dollar, dime, and cent. While his finances may increase or remain stable, may he never set his heart on them (Psalm 62:10), but rather count his wealth in things that cannot be bought. In Jesus' name, Amen.

30

PROTECTION
FOR THE DAY

Lord,
protect my husband today.
Hem him in behind and before,
and place Your hand over Him.

Amen.

(Psalm 139:5)

Psalm 34:22
Psalm 91:9-11
Psalm 18:1-3
Psalm 32:6-7
Psalm 121:7-8

ather, I thank You for the promises of safety You give throughout the Bible. You give us refuge. You are our strength and redeemer. Thank You that You will never leave us nor forsake us and that you will be gracious to us all the days of our lives.

Father, protect my husband in all the ways he walks; watch over his coming and going (Psalm 121:8), guiding him away from any harmful situations. Protect him from traveling accidents, work accidents, sicknesses, and harmful diseases of the body or mind. Protect him from violence and the people who do it. Lord, I know that Your arm is not too short that You cannot save (Isaiah 59:1). Preserve the life of my husband so that he might grow old to watch his children's children grow. I entrust him to You, fully convinced that You are able to protect him today and every day of his life (2 Timothy 1:12).

Father, when his heart is burdened and the world seems dark all around him, remind him that You are his shield, his deliverer, and his rock. Remind him that You are his firm foundation, cornerstone, and stronghold (2 Samuel 22:1-4). Protect him from any attacks the enemy plans to make on his mind and body by diverting the fiery darts that get sent his way. You will not fail him, for You will not reject Your people; You will never forsake Your inheritance (Psalm 94:14).

Father, I stand in the gap on behalf of my husband (Ezekiel 22:30-31), asking that You ash the blood of Jesus over him and our marriage that we may be protected spiritually and physically by Your great power and love. In Jesus' precious name, Amen.

31

A WORTHY EXAMPLE

Be imitators of God,
therefore, as dearly
loved children and live a life
of love, just as Christ
loved us and gave
Himself up for us
as a fragrant offering
and sacrifice to God.

Ephesians 5:1-2

Ephesians 4:31-32
1 Timothy 4:12
2 Timothy 2:15-16, 22-24

Dear Jesus, You have set a perfect example for us to follow; one of love, kindness, and humble obedience. Give my husband a desire to fashion his life after Yours, doing nothing out of vain conceit but considering others better than himself (Philippians 2:3). Remind him often that he has younger eyes watching him, looking up to him for guidance. Outside his home, remind him he has worldly eyes watching and needing an example of purity, goodness, and compassion for mankind.

Father, give him strength and courage to do his best to set a good example. Teach him that setting a respectable example includes watching the words he speaks, avoiding godless chatter, and having nothing to do with foolish and stupid arguments. Teach him that a man of good character sets an honorable standard when he refuses to quarrel, but instead is kind to everyone (2 Timothy 2:24).

Father, I pray my husband will leave a path worthy of following by the way he conducts himself. Remove any tendencies to be quick-tempered, for we know a man of quick temper does foolish things (Proverbs 14:17). Do not let him be foolish; remove any drunkenness, violence, dishonesty or any evil tendencies. In their place, teach him to be hospitable, and love what is good, to be self-controlled, upright, holy and disciplined. Help him live a blameless life, setting an honorable example (Titus 1:7-8).

Father, where my husband may have been less than exemplary, give him courage to repent and do better. I fervently pray that where a godly life has not been modeled for him, You would help him rise above and not fall into the traps of generations past. When he is unsure of the best thing to do, move his heart to dig into Your Word, the only good, right and perfect example for him to fashion his life after. In Jesus' name, Amen.

32

THE PATHS
HE WALKS

Lord,
impress Yourself
upon my heart,
that I may continually
walk in Your truth.

Amen.

Psalm 15:1-2
Proverbs 4:26-27
Micah 6:8
Philippians 3:13-15

ather, guide my husband's steps to walk in truth. Give him the courage to turn to right paths that lead *to* You and are led *by* You. May he be a man who learns to acclaim You and who walks in the light of Your presence (Psalm 89:15). I know You count blessed "the man who does not walk in the counsel of the wicked or stand in the way of sinners or sit in the seat of mockers" (Psalm 1:1). Today, convict and guide my husband away from any counsel that is not of You. Let him not take part in the activities of evil-doers, but rather have the courage to walk away from temptations.

Lord, we know "He who walks with the wise grows wise" (Proverbs 13:20). Send my husband along paths that will lead to relationships that help him grow wiser, more humble, and stronger in You. Father, teach my husband to be a man who will do what You require of him: "to act justly and to love mercy and to walk humbly" before You (Micah 6:8).

Lord, Your command to walk in love is not grievous. Give my husband a heart that is gentle and loving to all he meets today, letting his love for You shine bright and true. May he walk honestly and humbly, having a clear vision of the path You would have him take. Bless him with clarity and courage when You instruct him in his paths. Father, You move the hearts of kings, so You will also move the heart of my husband to walk and lead rightly, surely, and lovingly.

Encourage him not only to walk in truth, but also to do so quickly. Teach him to seek Your guidance first and foremost, knowing You will never mislead. May my husband abide in Your tabernacle and dwell on Your holy hill as he walks uprightly and works righteousness and speaks truth in his heart (Psalm 15:1-2).

At the end of his long life, Father, may he look back and praising You, say, "I have kept my feet from every evil path so that I might obey Your Word. I have not departed from Your laws, for You Yourself have taught me" (Psalm 119:101-102).

I pray You will continue teaching him to understand Your precepts and that he will hate every wrong path.

Strengthen his resolve to seek wisdom from Your Word: the very lamp to our feet and the light for our path (Psalm 119:105). May he always walk worthy of his calling, with all lowliness and gentleness, with long-suffering, and by bearing with all people in love (Ephesians 4:1-2). In Jesus' name, Amen.

Psalm 18:1-2

I love you, O Lord, my **STRENGTH**.

The Lord is my **ROCK**, my **FORTRESS**

and my **DELIVERER**;

my God is my rock,

in whom I take **REFUGE**.

He is my **SHIELD**

and the horn of my **SALVATION**,

my **STRONGHOLD**.

33

THE WORDS
HE SPEAKS

She speaks with wisdom,
and faithful instruction
is on her tongue.

Proverbs 31:26

Psalm 19:14
Colossians 3:8
James 1:19-20

Father, words are powerful. They carry life or death, blessing or curses, peace or dissension.

We know that out of the abundance of the heart the mouth speaks (Matthew 12:34). Make my husband's heart pure so that what comes out of his mouth is edifying to You. Do not let unwholesome talk come out of his mouth, but only what is helpful for building others up according to their needs (Ephesians 4:29).

Your Word tells us that there is more hope for a fool than a man who is hasty with his words (Proverbs 29:20). So when he feels like spewing anger or frustration, nudge his conscience and halt the words before they are uttered. Give him a gentle and patient spirit so that speaking kindly will become natural to him.

Grow the desire in him to think through his words before he speaks. I command away from his mind all negative thoughts that could result in unwholesome talk to others or about others. I take a stand against all evil spirits that encourage cussing, harsh words, uncaring words, or indifferent words. Give him the courage and strength to rid himself of anger, rage, malice, slander, and filthy language and to avoid godless chatter, knowing all those things will only lead to more ungodliness.

Instead of obscenity, foolish talk or coarse joking, convict him to speak in thanksgiving (Ephesians 5:4). Let his conversation always be full of grace, seasoned with salt, so he will always know how to answer everyone according to Your Word (Colossians 4:6). May the words of his mouth and the meditation of his heart be ever pleasing to You (Psalm 19:14). In Jesus' name, Amen.

COVERING
HIS CHOICES

Lord, help me
choose your instruction
rather than be swayed
by my thoughts
and feelings.

Amen.

Proverbs 16:1-3
Deuteronomy 28:13
Deuteronomy 30:9-10, 19-20

Father, once again I praise You that You have given my husband the ability to make wise choices based on Your Word. You have said, "I have set before you life and death, blessings and curses. Now choose life, so that you and your children may live, and that you may love the Lord your God, listen to Him and hold fast to Him" (Deuteronomy 30:19-20). Father, move my husband's heart to choose life and blessing every single day. Move him to choose Your instruction, knowledge, and wisdom instead of earthly riches and selfish gain (Proverbs 8:10).

Help my husband clearly see the way You would have him lead his family and live his life. May he boldly rise up and say, "as for me and my household, we will serve the Lord" (Joshua 24:15). Help him rise above present circumstances and see with an eternal perspective so he can make decisions based on Your will. If he makes a choice not glorifying to You, nudge his conscience to repentance.

All a man's ways seem right to him, but You, oh Lord, weigh the heart (Proverbs 21:2). Weigh my husband's heart and remove any offensive way in him that might hinder the choices he makes throughout his day. Keep his mind unobstructed when he is faced with decisions. Show him where he may be trusting too much in his own thinking rather than depending on You for guidance. Help him clearly confirm and accept the ways You want him to go.

Lord, I pray you will protect him from unhealthy pressures and expectations of this world that could drive him to make choices that ruin his mind, body, and soul. Direct his heart to say "no" to unhealthy relationships, harmful business deals, and selfish motivations. Supply him with wisdom so he may be kept in safety (Proverbs 28:26). In Jesus' precious name, Amen.

35

EVALUATING
FRIENDSHIPS

Jesus,
thank You for
being my friend that
sticks closer than a brother.

Amen.

(Proverbs 18:24)

Proverbs 16:28-29
Proverbs 20:19
1 Corinthians 15:33-34

Dear Jesus, You are our one forever faithful Friend. You are the One Who sticks closer than a brother (Proverbs 18:24), but You did not intend a man to walk this earth alone or without friends in human flesh and form. You have encouraged us to walk with the good and the upright so that we might not grow weary in doing good or grow weak and complacent in our faith. So, Father, today I pray my husband will seek out friends who are wise and gentle. Give him friends who, as iron sharpens iron, will sharpen him (Proverbs 27:17), who will encourage him to keep on in the faith and do what is good, honorable, and respectable.

May my husband always be cautious in friendships (Proverbs 12:26), not choosing company that would lead him down a path that is evil (Proverbs 16:28-29). Father, I pray You would remove any interest he might have in pursuing the activities and ways of ungodly friends. Give him wisdom to see where he may need to discontinue any friendship that is not uplifting to his character. Do not let him make friends with a hot-tempered or easily angered person, lest he learn to do the same (Proverbs 22:24-25). Give him the knowledge to know he needs to avoid anyone who talks too much, for such a person is prone to gossip and is not trustworthy (Proverbs 20:19).

Father, I pray my husband would be a man who attracts godly friends. Remind him to listen before he speaks and walk in the humility it takes to put others before himself. Do not allow him to expect from others what he doesn't expect from himself. Encourage him to be a friend like Jesus, be a man of integrity, not easily swayed by men, and paying no attention to their rank or name (Mark 12:14), but treating each person with dignity and respect. In Jesus' name, Amen.

36

HEALTH OF
BODY AND SOUL

Train yourself to be godly.
For physical training
is of some value,
but godliness has value
for all things.

1 Timothy 4:7-8

Proverbs 3:1-2, 7-8,
1 Corinthians 6:19-20
3 John 1:2

Father, You are the Healer who knows our bodies better than we do. Today, I pray that my husband's body will be kept in perfect harmony, working together and functioning the way You designed it to.

Father, help my husband take care of his body, for it is the temple where Your Spirit resides (1 Corinthians 3:16-17). I pray You would convict my husband to make healthy eating choices by not consuming anything that could harm or inhibit him from doing the work You have called him to do. Help him understand that he was bought at a price and he should honor You with his body (1 Corinthians 6:19-20). I pray he would not succumb to any food or substance addictions, but that in view of Your great mercy, offer his body as a living sacrifice, holy and pleasing to You (Romans 12:1).

Father, I pray also for his spiritual health. Urge him to obedience to Your Word, growing ever closer to You. Do not let him forget Your teaching, but convict him to store Your commands in his heart, for they will prolong his life and bring him prosperity (Proverbs 3:1-2). Let him not be wise as the world considers wise. I pray he will seek first to fear You and shun evil for that will bring health to his body and nourishment to his bones (Proverbs 3:7-8). Give him wisdom and the knowledge to understand that his first and foremost duty on this earth is to obey You and glorify You (Ecclesiastes 12:13).

I pray that my husband may enjoy good health and that all may go well with him, even as his soul continues growing well (3 John 1:2). Then, at the end of his long, obedient and good life, I pray he may cross over into Your presence gently, easily, peacefully, and joyfully. In Jesus' name, Amen.

HEALTHY EMOTIONS

Set your mind
on things above,
not on things that are
on this earth.

Colossians 3:2

Psalm 30:1-3
Psalm 31:3-5
Proverbs 16:32
Isaiah 61:3,7
Philippians 4:6-7

ather, I pray You would instruct my husband regarding his emotions. Help him understand that it is okay to feel and express his emotions in healthy ways.

I pray You would demolish all strongholds, removing any diseases of the mind or unhealthy emotional behaviors like anger, depression, indifference, fear, hopelessness or suicidal thoughts. Deliver him from any negative ways of thinking. Help him not be anxious about anything, but in everything give thanks (Philippians 4:6-7). When he feels depressed, remind him to call upon Your name so that he may find peace and great joy in Your presence. Redeem his soul; spare him from sinking him into the pits of despair (Psalm 30:3).

When my husband is frustrated, give him the wisdom and strength to control his words and actions. Do not let him be controlled by anger or fits of rage. Instead, renew in him a gentle, understanding spirit. I pray he would not be a jealous man who is always seeking but never finding, always wanting yet never content. Pour into his heart the emotions of thanksgiving and appreciation.

Father, free my husband from any shame he might have in showing sorrow, empathy, or any other emotions that others might not deem manly. Teach him also to enjoy the lighter moments so he isn't always weighted down by seriousness. Father, anoint him with Your oil of gladness (Isaiah 61:3). Renew him, strengthen him, and empower him against any effects negative emotions bring. In Jesus' name, Amen.

OVERCOMING HABITS

I can do all things
through Him
who gives me strength.

Philippians 4:13

Psalm 19:13
Peter 2:19
1 John 2:15-19
Galatians 5:1

Father, You have sent Your Holy Spirit to live in us. Our bodies are a temple, a place for us to meet with You. I pray my husband will not let anything consume his body or mind that could destroy this temple, for You have said, he who destroys Your temple You will destroy also (1 Corinthians 3:16-17).

I pray he will not be addicted to any harmful food or substance, nor participate in drunkenness or gluttony. I pray he will not be tempted to sin against his body by using or participating in pornography, sexual immorality, orgies, or the like. Keep his mind pure. Do not let him fall into the habitual ways of thinking that come from jealousy, anger, witchcraft, idolatry, or dissensions. Remove from my husband any tendency to gratify the flesh or seek self-satisfaction (Galatians 5:19-21). Do not let him be a man mastered by sinful desires (2 Peter 2:19). Instead, establish in him a clean heart with pure motives matched with the strength to stand against the enemy's temptations.

I stand humbly before You, Lord, asking that You keep my husband from any willful sin. Do not let him be ruled by his flesh (Psalm 19:13). Surround him with Your mighty protection. Lift him when he stumbles; carry him when he is weak. Strengthen him when he is tempted and convict him to persevere in what he knows is good, always growing into a greater faith. Remind him to be careful how he lives - not as unwise but as wise, making the best choice in every situation (Ephesians 5:15). After he has persevered, may he praise You, knowing he can do all things through Your Son who gives him strength (Philippians 4:13). In Jesus' precious name, Amen.

39

VICTORY OVER THE PAST

He heals the
brokenhearted
and binds up
their wounds.

Psalm 147:3

Ecclesiastes 7:10
Isaiah 42:9
Isaiah 43:18-19
2 Corinthians 4:16-18

Dear Jesus, thank You that You are able to set us free from all things past and present. You heal the broken-hearted and bind up their wounds (Proverbs 147:3). You have made a way for us to experience true freedom, and for that, I humbly thank You.

Bind up my husband's wounds, Jesus. Soothe his heart. Pour grace and mercy into him so that he may be able to forgive those who have hurt him. While it may be hard to forget what has been done to him, or what hasn't been done for him, I pray he would not lose heart but be strengthened day by day. Remind him that his troubles on earth are but momentary, so he may fix his eyes on You and cling tightly to Your great promises (2 Corinthians 4:16-18).

Father, You have told us to let go of former things and not dwell on the past (Isaiah 43:18-19). I pray my husband will not live in the past, or let it dictate him in any way. Instead, heighten his ability to do better for those coming after him than what was done for him. Strengthen him to stand against any generational sins that may be holding onto him. Help him see that You have a great and wonderful plan for him and You are calling him to set a new direction, a worthy heritage for his descendants.

Help my husband understand that You are capable of renewing all things, Father. That it is You who establishes a way through the desert and makes streams of life flow through wastelands of sin and pain. In Jesus' name, I stand against any powers and principalities of darkness that try to make him believe there is no hope. I lift my husband to You, trusting You to make him an over-comer. Though thousands would fall around him, in You he will remain unshaken.

Father, I pray that through my husband's complete deliverance, he would grow to find an appreciation for his past. May remembrances of his past serve only as reminders of Your great love and redeeming power, and result in praises to You for his healing and growth. May only peace, joy, thankfulness and greater faith come from the pains he has endured. Match and multiply the days of his gladness in proportion to his affliction (Psalm 90:15). In Jesus' name, Amen.

Prayers in Scripture

A PRAYER WHEN SEEKING GOD
Psalm 5:1-8

A PRAYER FOR DELIVERANCE
Psalm 71:1-12

A PRAYER FOR FAVOR
Psalm 17:1-9

A PRAYER FOR RESCUE
Psalm 69:13-18

A PRAYER FOR MERCY
Psalm 86:1-7

A PRAYER FOR JOY
Psalm 90:13-17

A PRAYER FOR HELP
Psalm 143:1-12

A PRAYER FOR A SETTLED SOUL
Psalm 46:1-11

A PRAYER FOR PERSONAL VICTORY
Psalm 18: 28-36

A PRAYER OF THANKSGIVING
Psalm 30:1-12

HOPE FOR
THE FUTURE

I have set the Lord
always before me.
Because He is at
my right hand,
I will not be shaken.

Psalm 16:8

Psalm 25:4-5
Psalm 26:2-3
Psalm 27:4-5

Father, thank You for this man You have set in my life. I pray You will give him a clear vision of what Your plan is for him. I pray that he will not pursue things of his own will but seek You first in all things, so he may lead his life in ways that are good, right, and beneficial to our marriage and our home.

Instruct him, Lord, in the way You would have him go. Stay at his right hand so he will not be shaken (Psalm 16:7). You have promised to give to each person that which he has done. I pray my husband will be a man who persistently seeks You in all he does and wherever He goes so that he may inherit eternal life (Romans 2:6-7).

Father, surround him with Your mighty wings, illuminate the path You would have him walk, and strengthen him to march courageously onward in obedience, whether the storm is favorable or unfavorable. I pray he would always be careful to live uprightly and act wisely, never letting an opportunity to bring glory to You go to waste (Ephesians 5:15-16).

Father, I lift my husband to You asking that You lead him in the way that is right so that it may go well with him, his marriage, and his descendants. In Jesus' precious name, Amen.

ABCs OF CHRISTIAN MARRIAGE

A marriage steeped in connection and trust is one of the most beautiful things on earth. So much so, that most of us would say there is no meaning, purpose or value in life if we don't have someone to share love, fears, failures and successes with; someone to know and be known by.

Someone to laugh with, cry with, love. The one we do life with. The one we still choose after we've experienced their worst. The one who still chooses us when we've demonstrated our failures.

Using the alphabet as a guide, we find words or phrases that encourage us to contribute value, meaning, and commitment to our marriage. Many of these are drawn from Bible verses, others are implied or just good old common sense. Enjoy!

ATTITUDE ADJUSTMENT

"Your attitude should be the same as that of Christ Jesus."

Philippians 2:5

To find a better understanding of what kind of attitude that is, you might consider reading Philippians 2:3-8.

BUILD EACH OTHER

"Let us therefore make every effort to do
what leads to peace and mutual edification."

Romans 14:19

"[E]ncourage one another daily, as long as it is called Today, so that none of you may be hardened by sin's deceitfulness."

Hebrews 3:13

"Therefore encourage one another and build each other up."

1 Thessalonians 5:11

CONTENT

"Do not say, "Why were the old days better than these?" For it is not wise to ask such questions."

Ecclesiastes 7:10

"[B]e content with what you have, because God has said, "Never will I leave you; never will I forsake you.""

Hebrews 13:5

DONATE YOUR EARS

"Everyone should be quick to listen, slow to speak and slow to become angry."

James 1:19

EJECT ANGER

"Get rid of all bitterness, rage and anger, brawling and slander, along with every form of malice."

Ephesians 4:31

FORFEIT GRUDGES

"Do not repay anyone evil for evil...Do not take revenge, my friends, but leave room for God's wrath, for it is written: "It is mine to avenge; I will repay," says the Lord."

Romans 12:17,19

"A heart at peace gives life to the body, but envy rots the bones."

Proverbs 14:30

GENTLENESS & KINDNESS

"Let your gentleness be known to all."

Philippians 4:5

"Be kind and compassionate to one another, forgiving each other, just as in Christ God forgave you."

Ephesians 4:32

HELP EACH OTHER

"Two are better than one, because they have a good return for
their work: If one falls down, his friend can help him up."

Ecclesiastes 4:9-10

INDUCE LOVE

"Be imitators of God, therefore, as dearly beloved children and
live a life of love, just as Christ loved us and gave Himself up
for us as a fragrant offering and sacrifice to God."

Ephesians 5:1-2

"Let no debt remain outstanding, except the continuing
debt to love one another, for he who loves his fellowman has
fulfilled the law. The commandments...are summed up in this
one rule: "Love your neighbor as yourself." Love does no harm
to its neighbor. Therefore love is the fulfillment of the law."

Romans 13:8-10

JOY TO ONE ANOTHER

"You have stolen my heart, my sister, my bride;
you have stolen my heart with one glance of your eyes...
How delightful is your love, my sister, my bride!
How much more pleasing is your love than wine."

Song of Solomon 4:9-10

"He seldom reflects on the days of his life,
because God keeps him occupied with gladness of heart."

Ecclesiastes 5:20

"Enjoy life with your wife (spouse), whom you love."

Ecclesiastes 9:9

KISS PASSIONATELY

"Let him kiss me with the kisses of his mouth—
for your love is more delightful than wine."

Song of Solomon 1:2

"Your lips drop sweetness as the honeycomb, my bride;
milk and honey are under your tongue."

Song of Solomon 4:11

LEAD YOURSELF WELL

In short, be responsible for yourself. You control your actions,
your words, all of you. Do it well and do it first.

"Do not think of yourself more highly than you ought,
but rather think of yourself with sober judgment."

Romans 12:3

MAKE UP

"If anyone has caused grief...you ought to forgive and comfort him, so that he will not be overwhelmed by excessive sorrow. I urge you, therefore, to reaffirm your love for him."

2 Corinthians 2:5-8

NOTICE EACH OTHERS NEEDS

"If anyone does not provide for his relatives, and especially for his immediate family, he has denied the faith and is worse than an unbeliever."

1 Timothy 5:8

ORGANIZE PRIORITIES

"But seek first His kingdom and his righteousness, and all these things will be given to you as well."

Matthew 6:33

"So we make it our goal to please Him, whether we are at home in the body or away from it."

2 Corinthians 5:9

PRAY

"And pray in the Spirit on all occasions with all kinds of
prayers and requests. With this in mind,
be alert and always keep on praying."

Ephesians 6:18

QUIET ARGUMENTS before they start

"A gentle answer turns away wrath,
but a harsh word stirs up anger."

Proverbs 15:1

"A hot-tempered man stirs up dissension,
but a patient man calms a quarrel."

Proverbs 15:18

R-RATED IS GOOD

Song of Solomon. That's all for this one!

SERVE EACH OTHER

"[S]erve one another in love. The entire law is summed up in
one single command: "Love your neighbor as yourself."

Galatians 5:13-14

THANKFUL FOR EACH OTHER

"I thank my God every time I remember you."

Philippians 1:3

UNDERSTANDING TOWARD EACH OTHER

"A patient man has great understanding."

Proverbs 14:29

"Love is patient...It always protects, always trusts, always hopes, always perseveres. Love never fails."

1 Corinthians 13:4-8

VERBALIZE FEELINGS APPROPRIATELY

Throwing around accusations that begin with "You always..." or, "You never..." is hardly beneficial to your spouse. It feels more like an attack. Telling your spouse how they've hurt you needs to be done kindly and calmly to avoid causing more pain.

"A man of knowledge uses words with restraint, and a man of understanding is even-tempered."

Proverbs 17:27

"Reckless words pierce like a sword,
but the tongue of the wise brings healing."

Proverbs 12:18

WISE WORDS

"The heart of the righteous weighs its answers,
but the mouth of the wicked gushes evil."

Proverbs 15:28

"She speaks with wisdom and
faithful instruction is on her tongue."

Proverbs 31:26

eXTEND GRACE

"He who loves a pure heart and whose speech is gracious
will have the king for his friend."

Proverbs 22:11

"A fool shows his annoyance at once,
but a prudent man overlooks an insult."

Proverbs 12:16

"A kindhearted woman gains respect."

Proverbs 11:16

YIELD YOUR RIGHT TO BE RIGHT

"Be completely humble and gentle;
be patient, bearing with one another in love.
Make every effort to keep the unity of the Spirit
through the bond of peace."

Ephesians 4:2-3

ZEALOUS FOR A LIFE TOGETHER

"Whether it is favorable or unfavorable,
we will obey the Lord our God...
so that it will go well with us,
for we will obey the Lord our God."

Jeremiah 42:6

kayleneyoder.com

ENJOY THIS EXCERPT FROM

a wife's 40-day Fasting & Prayer journal

Introduction

When I first started fasting for our marriage, I did so with the attitude, *that man has to change!* I was sure fasting was the magic wand that I could give a few flips and flings to and things would all straighten out.

I mean, the intent and promise for our fasting is to *"to loose the chains of injustice and untie the cords of the yoke...Then your light will break forth like the dawn, and your healing will quickly appear"* (Isaiah 58:6,8). What a great promise! And I wanted a piece of it.

Rewind a few years. The enemy had successfully sabotaged much of both our lives. Our marriage was painful, full of shattered dreams. My health was sliding downhill, and my faith was right behind it. I was in a desperate place. I longed for comfort and hope. The isolation, anger, disappointments, loneliness, and defeat were becoming too much.

I cried a lot. I prayed a little, not knowing if it was actually helping and wondering if there really was a God who gave two cents about me, where in the world was He and why didn't He show up? I screamed on inside at everything and on the outside at nothing.

My breaking point came one night as the brands of icy heartache once again pressed so deep I found it hard to breathe. Blinded by desperation for the healing of a painful marriage, I had it out with God. Barefooted, I ran for miles on gravel; I threw rocks at His sky, yelled, and when finally exhausted, I sat in His dirt refusing to move until He brought me some kind of relief. I didn't know what that relief looked like or whether it would come. Little did I care if it didn't as long as He would end the hurt and take me home with Him.

Yes, that was my prayer. Relieve me, or kill me. It was an Elisha moment from 1 Kings 19:4. But when my anger, frustration, and emotions were spent, and I was physically exhausted, the Lord surrounded me in ways only He can.

No words were spoken audibly, but I heard Him loud and clear. No touch that could be felt, but I knew I was being held. He comforted me, He quieted me with His love, and He gave me strength to simply breathe. There in the depths of anguish, the Comforter, Peace-bringer, Mighty God, Everlasting Father, Great Shepherd brought me to that comfort and rest that doesn't make sense.

There, nestled in the sacred ground beneath the wings of the One who loves you and me more than we can fathom, this book was born. There with the Lord, the stars, and the crickets, I knew I was called to do the greatest battle of my life- the battle for my marriage.

And it was going to be brutal. I was assured of that.

But it was going to be beautiful. I was even more assured of that.

The days, months, and years following have been harsh. Many times I've felt my will to keep pressing on falter. Many days my faith has been weak. Many days I would have preferred to curl up and let death set me free.

There are still days the enemy brings back past pains with such force it almost takes my breath away and leaves me whirling. However, the Lord hasn't brought us this far to let us become a statistic – of that, I am convinced. Greater is He who lives in us than he who lives in the world. We are made to conquer in the Lord, and when we bring all our brokenness to Him and dump it at His feet, He promises to care for us, fight for us, relieve us, nourish us, and carry us through. He doesn't mind if our anger, frustrations, pain, shame, distrust, and all manner of emotional breakdowns get unloaded on Him by the garbage truck full. He doesn't mind how bad it smells; He doesn't even mind if we do it in an undignified manner. He just desires that we bring it to Him. When we do, He proves His faithfulness. He proves Himself trustworthy. Faith is renewed, His power displayed, and His glory undeniable.

Dear friend, I don't know why you picked up this book. Maybe you are sitting in the unforgiving soil of a hard season. Maybe you are ready to make a run for it, ready to bolt, disappear, and never look back. Maybe you've grown distant and lonely in your marriage. Maybe you don't care whether your marriage is revived or not.

Maybe this fasting and prayer idea is your last resort.

If so, you are in good company. These next forty days have the capacity to change your marriage forever. The question remains: are you willing to go the distance? Are you ready to be molded, shaped and loved like never before?

Even though your answer may be a tentative 'yes,' I pray you will commit to taking just one day at a time. Keep in mind that Ephesians 6:10-18 tells us our battle is not with flesh and blood, but rather with the powers and principalities of darkness.

Our battle is with the enemy of our soul, not our husband. Our battlefield has greater proportions than just our marriage. The ultimate battle is for our faith. And if the enemy thinks he can get to our faith by attacking our marriage, you can put money on the fact that he is going to try it.

Stand strong, girlfriend.

By the end of this book, you will be glad you ran the race. You'll be better equipped to continue fighting the good fight. You'll be laser-focused on where your real battles are and Who to engage to fight for you. I pray you will not put this book on the shelf and forget about it. I pray this very book in your hands becomes rag-tag, written in, tear-stained, taped up, and tied together to keep it in place, not because of something I've written, but because of how the Lord moves you to greater dependency on Him and pulls you to greater intimacy and trust in Him.

I pray He continues to use this book over the many years of your marriage to snap the chains of oppression and untie the twines of sin. I pray that through consistent prayer and petition, the Lord will continue to satisfy your needs and soothe your pain just as He promises.

I believe when we call on Him, He will answer. I believe that He will always guide us and satisfy our needs in the deserts of life, that He will strengthen us, and as the Restorer of Broken Walls, will redeem the ruins of our lives and make them like well-watered gardens (Isaiah 58:6-11).

I don't know about you, but I could use a whole lot more of that.

So, join me. Let's do life from our knees for a while. Let's invite the mighty hand of God to sweep through our hearts, homes, and lives like never before, breaking through the walls, awakening our souls, cleansing our minds, ridding us of our self, then infusing us with Himself as He restores us for His glory. It's time to stake a few claims and retrieve the ground the enemy has stolen from our lives and our marriages.

Let's go, warrior friend!

Available at Amazon.com
and BarnesAndNoble.com

More from Kaylene Yoder

40 Scripture-Based Prayers
to Pray Over Your Wife

40 Scripture-Based Prayers
to Pray Over Your Children

A Wife's 40-Day Fasting & Prayer Journal
(devotional)

ABC Scripture Cards
for the Christian Marriage

Prayer Cards for
Husbands, Wives, and Parents

Prayer Challenges

R.E.S.T. Bible Study Method and Journals

and free printable resources can be found at:

https://kayleneyoder.com

Made in the USA
Coppell, TX
15 September 2021

62397735R00066